A Technique for Water Survival   DROWNPROOFING

A Technique for Water Survival

DROWNPROOFING

Michael Bettsworth

SCHOCKEN BOOKS · NEW YORK

First published by SCHOCKEN BOOKS 1977
Second Printing, 1977

Copyright © Michael Bettsworth 1976

Library of Congress Cataloging in Publication Data

Bettsworth, Michael
  Drownproofing.

   1. Drowning—Prevention. 2. Swimming. I. Title.

GV837.B46   1977   797.2'1   76-48762

Manufactured in the United States of America

Contents

Foreword

This small manual owes its existence to the generosity of Winchester College, and to the inspiration of my predecessor, Mr G. H. G. Dyson. In 1974 I was sent to the University of Alberta at Edmonton to learn all I could about drownproofing. There, under the expert tuition of Dr Murray Smith, I was convinced of the value of drownproofing in all water sports' programmes. Since then I have been in communication with representatives of most of our water sports governing bodies, and have received help and encouragement from all of them. In particular I owe a debt of gratitude to Mr Bob Bond of the R.Y.A., Mr Dickie Underwood of Loughborough College and Mr Norman Sarsfield of the A.S.A. These men have all pledged their support in one way or another to drownproofing. And their interest is important, for it should convince people that my aim is not to replace, but to supplement. Drownproofing must be seen in the light of all water activities, and it is for this reason that the book is a teaching guide, and not a philosophical treatise.

I have suggested where the skill fits into a water programme, but it has not been my intention to carry out a comparative study of water skills. Each person in the end will decide on his own priorities. This book is to allow him to decide with knowledge and personal, practical experience, for it is a sad fact that many in this country are woefully ignorant of what drownproofing is; yet they are prepared to venture erroneous opinions.

I acknowledge with gratitude the work of my photographer, Mr Dion de la Rue, and the patience of the many people who posed for photographs; particularly do I thank Mrs Pat Dixon.

Introduction

The aim of this book is two-fold. Firstly, I want to look at the meaning and implications of the word 'drowning', and secondly to suggest a method of training which will eliminate some of the factors discussed in that analysis.

We all have some idea of what we mean by drowning, and, indeed, of what we mean by swimming. However, any comparison we personally make between the two terms is often meaningless because we are thinking in terms of an event which probably did not happen in the way we think. Did X drown? Why did he drown? Could he not swim? These are questions which are always asked. By them we imply that, unless water conditions were so rough as to make any form of swimming impossible, he must have drowned because he could not swim. We carefully do not define what we mean by 'swimming'.

Longer thought on the subject may cause us to concede that a man may drown because he had too far to swim, or that he was encumbered by clothing, or that possibly he got cramp, or was injured. Obviously, we never know the answers to these questions because the person who has drowned cannot answer them. On the most up-to-date evidence I can find on the subject it has been possible to examine some of the likely events which lead up to the final 'death by water'.

I have fully examined the effects of cold, tiredness, injury and cramp and deduced from them facts which may allow us to make our water safety programmes safer. The result of this analysis is an even firmer conviction on my part of the value of drownproofing.

The book contains a full course of instruction in drownproofing useful for the teacher and taught alike. It is better, in my view, that the skill is taught by 'experts'. There are many sensations of 'feeling' which the teacher should have before embarking on a course for his pupils. The book will not of itself produce competent drownproofers. A diligent teacher may be able to go part of the way with the help of the book, but before he tries to teach the skill **he must have done it himself**. This emphasis is not a logical one in the acquisition of all physical skills. A coach need not be able to 'do' what his athlete can; he needs to be armed with principles and experience. A drownproofing teacher is dealing with a different kind of skill, and one which he must be able to master himself.

1 What is Drowning?

It is not uncommon to talk about the 'drowning' problem; we talk about it as we speak of the 'drinking' problem. That is, we imply that drowning or drunkenness are undersirable states of affairs about which we should 'do' something. But there is little similarity between the two problems as 'problems'. Drowning is in a very special category of problems. Of the 7000 or so drownings recorded annually in the United States, about 40 per cent are swimmers, people who voluntarily hazard their lives in the water and lose the wager. They need not do so, and we, the general public, soon forget about them. Drowning is pushed out of our mind because it is absolute. You cannot recover from drowning as you can recover from a brain haemorrhage. We cannot visit a drowned friend as we can one whose broken leg is mending.

THE CAUSES OF DROWNING

We have difficulty in defining drowning. Alcoholism is the action of alcohol on the human system; drowning is suffocation by water. But in the first case only the alcohol could have caused whatever side-effects ensued; in the second the water is only the last link in what may have been a long chain. When we talk about a drowned person we all assume we know what we mean. But do we?

A person drowns if he allows the water to win. He allows the water to win in the following ways:

1. *He cannot swim*. This brings its own problem of definition. Is the ability to swim 100 or 1000 metres in a swimming pool at school a sufficient test of swimming? In what way does the pool represent the conditions of sea, river or reservoir water? How does clothing hamper, or help, a swimmer? If we learnt to 'swim' at the age of 12 can we still 'swim' at 60? These are all questions which need to be asked when we talk about non-swimming, for even champion swimmers can fall victim to tides and currents. (See Fig. 1.)

2. *He becomes fatigued*. Our 'swimming ability' is useless to us if we are unable to keep it up for a sufficient time. It is

Figure 1   **A potential drowning. This sequence was taken as it happened. We were trying to establish facts about the relative floating positions of women of different builds and ages.**
a   **Note the woman furthest from the camera. She had not swum for many years and was out of practice. She is already working harder than the others.**
b   **She is now relaxed but sinking faster.**
c   **Stress point! She is tense and shortly takes in water.**
d   **She is being assisted to the side.**
e   **Safety!**

a | b
c | d
e

9

probable that more people become fatigued and then drown than simply drown. There are many factors which cause fatigue: rough water, heavy clothing, 'unfitness', age, shock, injury, cramp and cold. Any method of survival swimming must take in to account all these factors.

3. *He becomes cold.* Loss of inner core body heat (hypothermia) probably accounts for a large number of drownings. Exposure is known to sailors as well as to mountaineers. We know that major heat loss is from the chest, groin and particularly the head by conduction. It follows that anything which adds to the loss of heat from these places will hasten our demise. Work is going on to devise life jackets which will help to minimise heat loss, but not all who drown are sailors. We must ask ouselves what we can do for all categories of swimmers.

4. *He suffers from injury or cramp.* An injured swimmer will obviously get tired more quickly than a non-injured swimmer. This difficulty is usually compounded with an innate psychological response to injury or cramp which informs us that we are going to drown just because our swimming learning told us so!

5. *The above conditions are usually accompanied by shock.* Physiological and psychological response to shock is well known. An immediate drop in blood volume is a first response to neurogenic shock, and although this is soon remedied there is sufficient stress to cause cardio-vascular and cardio-respiratory inefficiency which will cause us to work harder, become tired, become colder, work harder . . . and drown. People's psychological responses vary. All we can say is that all people 'suffer' from shock. In our drowning situation there may be a host of other factors which add up to a vicious circle leading to eventual death.

6. *Large numbers of children die through negligence.* It must not be assumed that children die because they have gone swimming. A cursory glance at drowning statistics reveals that many children die because they were playing unsupervised *near* water. Likewise many yachtsman and others drown because they were not wearing lifejackets. No amount of survival training will save lives lost through negligence.

7. *Helplessness will obviously kill.* We cannot save a person who is held under the water or who has a heart attack with the shock of it all. There are some serious injuries which, if not treated in time, will cause death. However the most common drownings are unspectacular affairs, happening in apparently 'harmless' situations. Indeed most happen within 15 metres (50 feet) of safety.

OVERCOMING THE CAUSES OF DROWNING

1. *Inability to swim.* By re-defining our objective, we should say, perhaps, that a person can 'swim' if he can survive in moderately warm water, say 15°C, for an indefinite period of time whether he be injured or not. In order to be able to do this we must take another look at traditional concepts. We must question the validity of teaching all people to tread water or swim on the surface. It is easier to rest just below the surface and 'come up for air' than it is to hold 6.8 Kilogrammes (15 lbs) — the weight of a human head — out of the water. It is easier to separate the breathing and propulsive phases of 'swimming', than to combine the two. In short, it is easier to drownproof than to learn traditional skills if we are talking about survival. But **drownproofing is no substitute for swimming**. It is not a panacea which will guard us against all water difficulties. It is a useful additional skill.

2. *Fatigue, cold, injury and cramp.* Tiredness and exposure are both caused by heavy exertion. They are part and parcel of the same thing. If we swim around madly in cold water we lose heat from the 'centre' of the body, as well as using up vital sources of energy — heat — which will keep us warm. Therefore it is far better to learn to be completely static in water if we are likely to be in it for a long time or if it is very cold and our length of immersion is unknown. Similarly we should keep clothing on: warm water will be trapped between the clothing and the skin and act as an insulator; strong movements will cause this warm water to be replaced by colder water and the effect is lost. Thus cold, clothing, and tiredness are inter-related.

If our survival skill — our answer to the problem — rests with economy of effort in order to conserve body heat and lessen the effects of shock, so too must it take into account the problem of limb immobilisation. It is useless to be able to swim front crawl like an Olympic champion if as soon as one arm is broken we are likely to drown. A skill which can be performed, if necessary, with no limbs at all is what is sought. Drownproofing is such a skill. It can be done while one is tied up, by polio victims and limbless people.

CONCLUSION

For the purposes of this book our ideal is to teach a technique which reduces the effects of cold, can be done by an injured as well as a fit person, can be done with a minimum of effort, and which does not depend for successful accomplishment on prior conditioning or comparative youth.

In isolating the distinctive qualities of drownproofing it must be constantly emphasised that this technique is not the sole answer to the drowning problem. The place of the technique in an overall swimming programme is no more or less important than life saving or water polo.

As a survival skill it adds to the existing skills a different emphasis. The drownproofing rest position is not a replacement for treading water. Drownproofing *per se* does not deal with underwater swimming or surface diving. In short it takes its place along side all the other skills as an interesting and valuable addition. Its practical relevance may relate to less than one per cent of drowning cases — it has that in common with all survival skills. Its advantage is that it goes some way to preparing for the extreme emergency — excessive cold, limb immobilisation and so on.

From an educational point of view the satisfaction of surviving in deep water while your hands and legs are tied is great, just as is the sense of achievement great after swimming a thousand metres or floating on inflated clothing. All experience is valuable to a child. Some experiences have an extrinsic as well as an intrinsic value. Drownproofing is one such.

a

Flotation and of Drownproofing

An ability to swim by any definition requires us to master the principles of buoyancy and propulsion. We can only swim because the water wholly or in part supports our body mass.

Iron and wood do not 'sink' when placed on, say, a table top. This is because the particles which make up the table top do not move aside to allow the iron to pass through. If iron is placed in water or air the particles in these elements can move aside, so that an object heavier than them, bulk for bulk, sinks. Thus a piece of iron sinks through water and through air , but a piece of wood does not sink through water — it will through air — because a given volume of wood is lighter than the same volume of water, but heavier than the same volume of air.

What determines whether an object floats is whether the weight of a given volume of the object is heavier or lighter than the equivalent volume of the fluid. A cubic metre of iron sinks in water because it weighs more than a cubic metre of water. That is, it contains more matter than that in a similar volume of water; the matter constituting iron being denser than that constituting water. The relative density of iron is greater than that of water. If the density of water is taken as 1, the relative

Figure 2   **The man and the woman have filled up with air and then stopped doing anything with their limbs.**
a   **Both have sunk — but note how much deeper the man is.**
b   **After four or five seconds both have risen — the man is still deeper.**

density of iron is 7.8. The relative density of sea water, because of the presence of dissolved mineral salts in it, is 1.0275. This explains why it is easier to float in salt than in fresh water.

The weight of any substance, or the force of gravity upon it, is directly proportional to its relative density, hence the term specific gravity is used to denote the ratio of the weight of a substance to that of an equal volume of pure cold water.

We can only float if our specific gravity is less than that of water. In practice 99.9 per cent of all women will float if they are full of air. 99 per cent of men will do the same. The difference between the sexes is that men are denser than women. Bone and muscle have a specific gravity greater than 1. Fat and air do not. Bone and muscle sinks, fat and air float (see Fig. 2). Provided the combined specific gravity of the elements is less than 1 the object will float. The element common to all is air. Just as an iron ship floats because its volume is made up of light objects or spaces full of air, so will the human body float better if all its available space (the lungs) is full of air. If despite the air in the lungs a body sinks, then one must create an upthrust to counterbalance the effects of gravity. In swimming this is done with the legs and arms and produces a forward as well as an upward motion. (It is of value to remind readers here that a relaxed swimmer will float more easily than a tense one. The contraction of the muscles will cause one to become denser.)

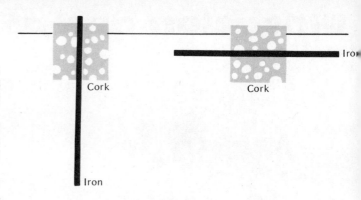

Figure 3

From what has been said above it follows that fat men will float better than thin men or muscular ones. Similarly thin or heavily built women will float less efficiently than their less dense counterparts. The age and sex of a person is relevant here only insofar as the distribution of fat, bone, muscle and air is concerned.

The distribution of bone, muscle and fat in the body will ultimately determine the floating position of the body. Legs are made up of large bones and because of their daily locomotive function a large amount of muscle. Legs sink! With most people the natural floating position of the body is vertical. Some women are able to remain afloat horizontally without effort as are very fat men. It is very noticeable in legless people that they float far more horizontally than their able-bodied counterparts.

The diagram (Fig. 3) shows the mechanical process involved when a man relaxes from the horizontal floating position. The weight of his legs represents the iron not in the cork. The cork — less dense than air — approximates to the lungs and the less dense upper body parts. The body rotates around its centre of gravity until it reaches a state of equilibrium. The position of the centre of gravity depends upon the length and weight of the legs, the distribution of fat, etc. One can think of it as the point around which the whole body pivots — the whole weight of the body appears to act from it. Notice the difference in the centres of gravity (see also Figs. 8 and 9, pp. 24, 25 and 26).

Many people think they cannot float because they have not been taught an efficient technique. To most of us the word 'floating' conjures up a picture of lying on one's back, toes out of the water reading a book while smoking a cigar and drinking gin! In practice very few people float like that.

Just as with the term 'swimming' so with that of 'floating' do we have to redefine what we mean. Most men are incapable of floating on their backs without their legs dropping and once the legs have dropped we can only remain afloat by treading water — or so we think. A logical look at this process yields a peculiar picture. The average head weighs 6.8 kg (15 lbs). In treading water most of this is being held above the surface. That is, we are having to do enough work to lift 6.8 kg in weight. The process of lifting has a reaction — Newton works even when he

Figure 4   **Treading water. The man is having to work hard to keep his head out of water.**

is wet — and this reaction is a downward one. We are, then, performing the initial skill of holding the head up, and as a reaction to this action having our work load increased by the compounding of the initial anti-gravity task with its self-produced reaction. Stated thus the absurdity of treading water in a survival situation is obvious. In the photograph (Fig. 4) the girl is doing the more sensible thing; her chin is in the water, but look at the man. His chin, shoulders and half his chest is out of the water! He will probably tell us that it makes it easier for him to breath in that position! It certainly will not make it any harder!

Breathing is very easy when the head is clear of the water all the time you will say. Ignoring the difficulty of breathing under water without the use of gills, are either the man or woman in the picture doing the most sensible thing? The fatigue which comes upon us when we tread water for any length of time causes us to puff and pant — particularly if we are very bad floaters and in cold water. Inefficient breathing means that we must work harder to keep afloat because our fuel stocks are limited. Eventually we begin to take in water, we work harder to take in less water become more fatigued . . . we are in the same vicious circle as before. The problem becomes more acute if we hope to travel in the water as we breathe. Drownproofers overcome this technical problem by separating breathing from propulsion. They also do not recommend holding the weight of the head out of the water unnecessarily. 'Unnecessarily' because the water will hold it for you! In conventional swimming we are working **on** the water. In drownproofing we are working **in** the water. We lift arms **up** and **out** of the water in most strokes. In drownproofing everything stays in the water except the head, and that only comes up during the inhalation.

The above may seem a damning indictment of traditional swimming techniques. What I am suggesting is less extreme. I argue that in the context of survival swimming traditional methods are uneconomical and often unrealistic. They may serve the fit young man or the fat old one; but on the whole they will not help old people, sinkers, or those who are injured. But far from denigrating swimming I am seeking to suggest that swimming is a far greater achievement than is generally recognised. We cannot all become champion swimmers however hard we train. But we can all become champion drownproofers with no 'training' only some practice. We cannot all answer the challenges set by national organisations; if we could they would cease to be challenges, but we are all so accustomed to the concept of traditional stroke technique, to survival swimming and lifesaving tests as a part of our national culture that we are *blasé* about the water. A child who cannot pass her 'bronze' is a 'weak' swimmer. A child who has an 'Honours' award is a 'strong' swimmer. It would seem that they have nothing in common in the water. In fact they have two things identical. One is that they are both capable of drowning easily. The other is that they are both capable of learning drownproofing easily.

3 Drownproofing

HISTORY

The technique was devised in America by the late Fred Lanoue who was Associate Professor of Physical Education at the Georgia Institute of Technology. During the Second World War he realised that more American servicemen were losing their lives by drowning than were being killed in combat. He set himself the task of finding out how this appalling loss of life could be cut.

Initially Lanoue was dealing with a certain type of swimmer. His subjects were male, young and, because of their combat training, fit and muscular — traditionally a poor bet in the floating and swimming stakes. Many of these men could be classified as 'sinkers' — that is men who when full of air and resting on the surface of the water continue to descend. Others were total non-swimmers. Furthermore Lanoue did not have much time in which to teach these men a survival skill. There were two things in his favour; the first was that the men were used to obeying orders, and the second was that they were highly motivated. The technique he devised was gloriously simple.

PRINCIPLES

Using the common knowledge of the buoyant properties of water as his main consideration — and not just as a useful secondary consideration — and knowing that the water created an upthrust equal to the downward pressure of the body mass, Lanoue reasoned that this upthrust, when harnessed to the human ability to float, would solve his problem. Even if some swimmers were not very buoyant in their own right, he realised that a simple leg or arm action would allow even the poorest floaters to remain on the surface. Once these men's negative buoyancy was overcome they could not only remain afloat, but also travel. Lanoue was also armed with the vital information concerning cold, injury and fatigue mentioned above.

Once a person could stay afloat in a relaxed way it was easy to teach them to drownproof. But first they had to be taught to float face downwards in a vertical position, because that is the position which the water dictates (see p. 26), and Lanoue was training people to work with the water. This position also makes breathing easier over an extended period of time. The folly of holding one's head permanently out of the water has been discussed in Chapter 2. Using the face down position Lanoue trained swimmers to breath only about five or six times a minute. The energy conserved by lifting the head only when one wants to breathe is considerable. However, the action of lifting the head causes a reaction which tends to send the body downwards; a simple compensatory kick solves this problem for the poor floater. It will be quickly discovered that a trained swimmer can breathe and travel in the water with only a minimal use of any limbs. This is a vital consideration in the case of the physically handicapped or injured swimmer.

Lanoue additionally devised a simple travel stroke in which he separated the breathing and propulsive phases of the stroke. In traditional swimming the two aspects are combined; there are those who find it difficult to combine the two. Lanoue got rid of this difficulty. Thus a swimmer who wants to travel does so by gliding face downwards, then, when he wants to breathe, stops and goes through the breathing cycle.

In principle, then, the skill is a simple one. Its success depends upon the ability of a person to relax in the water and let it do the work. This is a completely different approach from that used in the physically demanding, more traditional activities. The basic principle is to 'come up for air'.

APPLICATION

Drownproofing is a self-survival skill. It is not a magical formula which will save life irrespective of water conditions. But it does offer a person a good chance of survival provided he is not in Arctic waters, or severely injured or being held under water.

It is a skill which should be taught alongside all other water skills and should be regarded as a very valuable additional technique. All adults should learn it, but it is not necessarily the skill children should learn first; knowledge of the principles of flotation mentioned in Chapter 2 is essential to the mastering of the technique. However, most children over the age of about nine can master it easily after a few hours' instruction. Non-swimming adults should learn the skill first; it gives them the security they need at once.

The descriptions and diagrams below show the breathing cycle and travel stroke *in toto*. A full, step-by-step description of how to do the skill is in the next two chapters.

THE BREATHING CYCLE

Stage 1: Vertical Rest
(a) Take a deep breath; sink vertically.
(b) Relax the entire body, let the chin drop to the chest, arms hang.
(c) If water enters the mouth, cough it out underwater.

Stage 2: Ready Position
(a) Leisurely cross arms in front of forehead, angling palms outward, forearms together.
(b) Raise one knee to chest; raise and extend the other foot behind in stride position (this is unnecessary for most people except sinkers).
(c) Keep the head horizontal with the back of the head out of the water.

Figure 5   **The breathing cycle.**

Stage 3: Exhale
(a) Gently raise the head breathing out all the time. Stop while the chin is still in the water.
(b) Fully open eyes out of the water. The rest of the body is still in the ready position.

Stage 4: Inhale
(a) Gently sweep arms out and down while stepping down on the water with both feet. Breathe in normally.

Stage 5: Fall Back Under Water

Stage 6: Resume Vertical Rest Position
(a) Legs are together after inhaling; let the arms drop to the hanging position as you sink in the water.
(b) As the head sinks below the surface, relax the neck and let the chin drop. Start to repeat the cycle.

1 2 3 4

Figure 6   The travel stroke.

THE TRAVEL STROKE

Stage 1: Begin at Stage 5 of Breathing Cycle

Stage 2: Recovery
(a) As head submerges, tip it forward and open legs to the ready position.
(b) Extend arms, hands together, in front of head.

Stages 3 and 4: Kick and Pull
(a) Kick the legs together and glide.
(b) At the end of this glide sweep arms backwards and glide again.
(c) Keep hands by thighs and relax, head down in the water.
(d) As body glides, gently exhale through the nose.

4   5   6   7   8

Stage 5: Vertical Rest
Return to the vertical position by bowing back and lifting knees towards chest.

Stages 6, 7 and 8: Resume Breathing Cycle
When vertical use drownproof method for breathing. Alternate one drownproofing breathing cycle to one travel stroke cycle.

4 The Breathing Cycle

The methods outlined in this chapter and the next will work for almost all men, women and children. The special problems encountered by sinkers, non-swimming adults, the physically handicappéd and those wearing buoyancy aids are discussed in Chapter 6.

THE FLOATING POSITION
The basic requirement is confidence in the water which will enable the learner to relax. This confidence is quickly achieved when the learner not only realises that the water will hold him, but also why it will support him. The following practices are aimed at giving the learner both understanding and confidence.

TREADING WATER
1. Learners should start by treading water in any way they can. Despite the uneconomical way of working this entails, they will be keen to do this in the beginning. The chin and shoulders must be kept in the water (see Fig. 4, p. 15).
2. Repeat (1) but use the minimum force required to keep the mouth clear of the water.

Common Faults
Not settling down into the water but fighting to keep the maximum body area above the water line. This is a tiring practice and the learner needs to know that 'the higher he is,

the harder he will fall' back into the water. Explain that the water should be doing most of the work.

3. Ask the learners to inhale fully and stop working. They will find they submerge a little way then stop going down. Notice in Fig. 2 (p. 12) how much deeper the man sinks into the water than the woman. Most people will float up to the surface without any effort provided they hold on to the position for a few seconds. Sinkers will experience trouble, but most people will be able to propel themselves back to the surface with a gentle leg action.

Common Faults
In all these practices novices will heave themselves out of the water to make sure that they sink! This is a tacit admission on their part that in order to sink they have to fight the water's buoyancy. They must just 'flop' when told to let go, and see what happens.

4. Repeat (3) but with empty lungs. Learners will realise that their rate of descent is much faster. Incidentally they will have no difficulty coming up to the surface again using their legs. Repeat the practice until they can come to the surface gently so that the chin does not break the surface.

By the end of a few minutes' practice learners will be

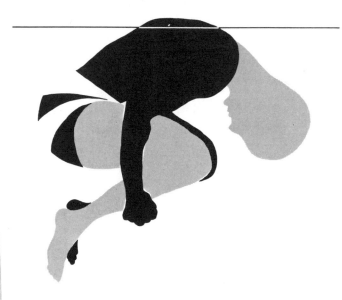

Figure 7   **The mushroom float.**

THE MUSHROOM FLOAT

This is one of the easiest ways of floating. Take a breath and place the face in the water clasping the knees to the chest (Fig. 7). The body will float with the back breaking the surface of the water. It will easily be seen that this is a natural floating position akin to the drownproofing position. Make the point about the weight of the legs being an obstacle to floating — hence they are tucked up here. Tell learners to concentrate on feeling cold air on their exposed backs.

THE JELLYFISH FLOAT

Stand chest deep in the water with the feet wide apart. Take a breath and slide the hands down the legs and grasp the ankles. Avoid falling backwards or forwards and the body will rise to the surface.

THE DROWNPROOFING FLOATING POSITION

Once a learner has realised his buoyancy potential it is time to continue. Many people believe that if you turn on your back you will float. In fact it is rare to find women and even rarer to find men who can float on their backs without using their hands for sculling. It is useful to start with an exercise which will show learners that they cannot back float since the position their bodies will take up is the first step towards the drownproofing position (Fig. 8).

beginning to relax and work with the water, or they will be exhausted through trying to fight the water. It is important to persist until confidence and relaxation are achieved.

1. Tell the learners to float on their backs in any way they can. They will all be working with their hands to maintain the position. Tell them to stop using their hands and see what happens. The weight of the legs will cause the body to become vertical.
2. Repeat (1) but when they are near the vertical position lift the head and take a breath. When the head is back under water, not before, look to the bottom. The eyes should be open, the neck relaxed and the chin nearly on the chest. Let the arms hang down and relax the legs. The position should now be similar to that shown in Fig. 9.

a

d

Figure 8   Finding the natural floating position.
a   The man and the woman both start floating on their backs in a horizontal position. Note that the man is already dropping.
b   Two seconds later.
c   The man is nearly in the vertical rest position; the woman is not yet vertical.
d   The man is now in the vertical rest position; the woman is vertical.
e   The man's position is unchanged; the woman is nearly in the vertical rest position.
f   The final floating position is determined by each individual's buoyancy; notice how much nearer the horizontal the woman is. Notice also the position of the heads.

24

b

c

e

f

Figure 9

Those who continue to descend may need to do a compensatory leg or arm action (see p. 47 for sinkers). Women and young boys will float less vertically than most men, but remember that it is the water's job to determine in which position a person will float. All the learners must be able to 'feel' their legs and arms dangling, and be aware of cold air on the exposed part of their back. This stage must be reached before continuing.

Common Faults
Eyes are closed and the head is thrown forward upsetting the whole poise. The body is not relaxed. To correct this, repeat the practice until the learner feels relaxed enough to be able to shake his legs, arms and head about without losing the position. If he can do this he is relaxed. Emphasise that the water will determine each person's floating position.

At this stage explain why the head should be looking down:

(a) the water will be supporting it and the neck is relaxed;
(b) breathing is easier from a face-down position because the neck muscles have only to lift the head until the mouth is out of the water. If the head is already vertical there will be a tendency for the body to sink anyway, and then

breathing can occur easily only if the head is thrown backwards.

3. Repeat (2) above from the vertical position, continuously, breathing when necessary. Try to avoid treading water too much at this stage as this is tiring. Remember when the head is submerged to relax the neck and look down. Keep the eyes open. Learners who do not feel confident that they will surface may do one gentle leg kick.

Common Faults
● *A too hard kick which lifts the shoulders out of the water and causes deeper sinking back into the water.*
● *Looking down too soon. Bending from the hips.*

If the learner has successfully completed the requirements above he is in the drownproofer's floating position. He will have seen that the position is the natural floating position of the body, and that it is a very relaxing one.

He must continue to practise the movement until he can do it without the shoulders or chin coming out of the water. Up to this stage learners will have been breathing at will. Once the learner feels confident that he will float up to the surface with or without help from his arms or legs, he must regularise his breathing.

THE BREATHING CYCLE

1. In the rest position (see Figs. 10a and 11), bring the arms slowly up to the forehead, thumbs leading the way (10b). Take the forearms to the forehead so that the palms are angled downwards and each palm is level with the elbow of the opposite arm (Fig. 10c). At this point sinkers and the less confident may need to do a scissor kick with their legs (10d).
2. Lift the head **gently**, breathing out all the while. Keep the chin and shoulders in the water. When the mouth has broken the surface, sweep the arms firmly outwards and sideways, and in the case of those using their legs, press down on the water with the feet, and breathe in (10e). The arm and leg action will 'hold' you in the water long enough to be able to take an adequate breath (10f).
3. When the arms have reached their downward sweep at the end of stage 4 sink back into the water. When the head is submerged look down again. You will be back in the rest position. Repeat the cycle for three minutes.

Common Faults
● *Lifting the arms too vigorously and in an 'unstreamlined' position. This will cause you to sink even before you have taken a breath.*

a

b

c

Figure 10   The breathing cycle.
a   The vertical rest position.
b   Raising the arms to prepare for the arm action. Note the thumbs leading the way.

c   The forearms are up to the forehead, the legs are scissored' in readiness for the breathing action.

d

e

f

d   The legs are pressing down on the water (good floaters will not need to use their legs); the head is being raised and exhalation is occurring.

e   The mouth is now clear of the water and inhalation is taking place. The arms are sweeping downwards and sideways to support the body at this stage; the legs are still providing support as well.

f   Breathing has taken place. The arms have finished with the hands touching the thighs. The head is coming back into the water.

g   The body has regained the relaxed vertical rest position.

a

b

Figure 11   The breathing cycle from above.
a   The arms are ready for their sweep downwards. Notice how the back
of the head is out of the water and the legs hanging down. This position
is almost as relaxing as with the arms hanging down.
b   The same position but with the legs ready to provide extra support
for those who need this. Notice the position of the arms.

- *Throwing the head back and causing the body to sink.*
- *Not completing the exhalation by the time the head breaks the surface; This may mean that there is unsufficient time for complete inspiration to occur.*
- *A too forceful arm sweep or leg 'kick' will leave insufficient time for a breath to be taken, and will also cause you to sink deeper into the water than necessary, because the shoulders and chest are likely to have been lifted clear of the water. The deeper you sink the harder you will have to work in order to assume the rest position. Over a period of time fatigue will set in.*
- *Sculling with the hands to allow more time to breathe. From the outset learners must be allowed only* **one** *arm sweep and* **one** *intake of breath.*
- *If insufficient breath has been taken in learners are tempted to tread water to make up for the deficiency. This practice will prevent their ever learning the breathing cycle and must be stopped.*
- *Putting the head back into the water too quickly and upsetting the control of the movement.*
- *Beginners often fail to bring their forearms up to their foreheads. They bring fingertips to fingertips and, hence, halve the length of their arm sweep which results in a halving of the time in which to take a breath.*

The teacher should emphasise that the learner breathes when he **wants** to and not when he has to and only a **normal** breath should be taken. The head should remain in the water except during the exchange of breath, and then it should only come out once to allow only **one** breath. Watch out for tensing of the arms and legs during the rest phase. Allow only one arm or leg action during the intake of breath, and as a compensatory movement for poor floaters. In general remind learners that drownproofing's major advantage is that it is an economical way of working. Every extra movement is extra work.

In the early stages of the above practice people experience an unpleasant tightness in the chest, and feel as if their lungs are bursting. The cause of this is two-fold. Firstly, they are probably taking in more air than they need. Secondly, they are probably holding onto their breath longer than is necessary or comfortable. Re-emphasise that breathing should be normal for they should not be exerting themselves. As time goes on the skill becomes easier and easier to do. The amount of air each person needs can only be discovered on a trial and error basis. Experimentation will soon decide.

It is vital at this stage that the learner does not compensate for the feeling of discomfort by treading water until 'he has got his breath back'. If he does this he will never learn the skill. It is the hard fact that if he swallows water he must pretend he has taken in air, and carry on. If he misses a breath he must do better next time around. If he takes in too little air he must make up for the loss next time around. If the initial discomfort is endured — and everybody has it — the learner will soon be in a rhythm with no problems at all.

Each time the cycle is practised set a limit. Start with, say, five cycles and work up to ten minutes. This is one of the classic cases of practice making perfect. The learners may need to be encouraged into enduring the intial discomfort; once they have done half a dozen cycles they will improve rapidly.

ADVANCED PRACTICE

Once a learner can do the breathing cycle for ten minutes he becomes bored! By this stage he has mastered the breathing cycle, and will have noticed that he can comfortably hold his breath longer under water than he could previously, and that he seems to be floating better and better. In an almost magical way the skill becomes easier and easier to do the longer one perseveres, such that even poor floaters will find that after a few minutes' successful practice they will come up to the surface with virtually no effort from arms or legs. The secret of this success lies in the ability to relax which has been emphasised so much previously. Our drownproofer is now ready to test his new-found confidence. The following exercises are both enjoyable and teach the value of drownproofing in situations where one or more limbs may be immobilised by injury.

1. If the learner has been doing a compensatory leg kick to bring him up to the suface he can try to do the skill by locking his legs together and using only his arms in the breathing cycle. His legs will not be so relaxed in this position, but once he is confident that he does not need to use them he can let them hang in the position the water dictates.

Common Faults
He will be less relaxed to start with and over compensate by pulling too vigorously with his arms. Remind him that the shoulders and chin should remain in the water.

2. If (1) above has been successfully completed he may like to try and do the skill using no arms (Figs. 12 and 13). He will enter the water and place his arms behind his back (Fig. 12, stage 1). The breathing cycle is that used for sinkers (see Chapter 6) except that he will not use his arms. Adopt the scissors position with the legs and at the same time raise the head breathing out while doing so (stages 2 and 3). When the mouth breaks the surface breathe in and at the same time press down on the water with the feet so that the body position is held long enough for breathing to occur (stage 4). With the feet together sink back under the surface. If at this stage the learner finds that he is sinking too far under he may do one gentle scissor kick to bring him back

up to the rest position. Repeat for three minutes.

Common Faults
● *A too vigorous leg action which brings shoulders and chin out of the water.*
● *Throwing the head back and causing the body to sink before inspiration can occur.*

Figure 12   **The breathing cycle with the arms immobilised.**

● *Not looking to the bottom of the pool when the head has submerged.*
● *Closing the eyes.*
● *Taking more than one breath.*
● *Too many leg kicks.*

33

All the above faults will sort themselves out as the practice proceeds. The teacher must be aware of them, but particularly must ensure that the learner does not kick his legs more than once during the breathing and recovery phases. Any additional muscular movement is unnecessary and fatiguing. The learner should, at this stage, have full confidence in the water's buoyancy. If the learner cannot do this skill after a couple of minutes' practice he is not ready for it.

3. The breathing cycle without the use of arms or legs. The learner enters the water and places his arms behind his back and locks his legs together. He assumes the rest position. He breathes out while lifting his mouth clear of the water. When the mouth is clear he breathes in and lowers himself back into the water. All movement must be **very gentle**.

Common Faults
- *Throwing the head back.*
- *Sinking too far into the water. If, in the early stages of the exercise, the learner feels he has to wait too long before assuming the rest position he can do one or two gentle dolphin leg kicks to bring him up. Similarly he can use his legs this way when he breathes.*

Initially the learner will be insufficiently relaxed in order to take in enough breath. He will throw his head back, etc. Try to continue the practice even if he has taken in water. After a few cycles he will find that all is going well and he need no longer use his legs even to give him more time in which to breathe. Watch out for learners who hold onto their breath until the last minute. Remind them that they breathe when they want to.

TYING UP THE LEARNERS
If the foregoing skills have been achieved the learners may ask if you will tie them up. Some teachers live a long time before that sort of opportunity occurs! But with drownproofing. . . . Use rubber tubing as this expands easily and the learner will feel confident that if he is in difficulty he can easily 'escape'. The inner tubes of bicycle tyres are most readily available. It is not necessary to tie the tubing into a knot, although I use bands of two sizes which have been previously tied; one for legs and one for ankles. The bands do not need to be tight.

WHENEVER A LEARNER IS IN THE WATER HE MUST HAVE A RESPONSIBLE PARTNER ON THE POOL SIDE SUPERVISING HIM AT ALL TIMES.

1. Tie up the legs and the learner does the breathing cycle for three minutes as he did in the first advanced practice (Fig. 13).
2. Tie up the hands and do the breathing cycle for sinkers for three minutes. The subject must enter the water unaided.

a

b

c

Common Faults
The same faults as exercise (2) on page 33.

It will be seen that whenever a learner is tied up wholly or partly he will become tense. The tension goes if he perseveres with the initial strange feeling. Learners who find serious difficulties are probably not sufficiently advanced to do this practice.

Figure 13   The breathing cycle with the arms tied. Constant supervision from the pool side is essential.
a   From the vertical rest position, the woman has prepared her legs for the scissor kick.
b   The legs are kicking gently but firmly, and the head is being raised.
c   By the end of the kick the mouth is clear and breathing is taking place. Notice that the chin is still in the water. From this position, resume the vertical rest and repeat the cycle.

a

b

c

Figure 14   The breathing cycle with the arms and legs tied. Constant supervision from the pool side is essential.
a   The vertical rest position.
b   Preparing to breathe.

c   The mouth is clear of the water; the legs prepare to kick downwards to counteract the tendency of the body to sink when the head is raised.

d   The legs have kicked and breathing in has taken place.

e   The body is sinking back into the water. The legs are kicking to prevent too deep an immersion.

f   The vertical rest position is resumed.

3. With hands tied behind his back the subject locks his legs together and drownproofs for three minutes.
4. Tie up arms and legs. The learner must enter the water unaided. **Supervision must be meticulous.** Drownproof for three minutes (Fig. 14).

Common Faults
By this stage there are few faults. Learners enjoy the feeling of confidence and ease with which they rest in the water. Breathing is done with a gentle raising of the head. Any tendency to sink is easily compensated for by a gentle dolphin leg kick.

All the above practices can be done by fully dressed swimmers. It does not take long for a swimmer to be able to counteract the effect of the clothing; some, even in a swimming pool, prefer the extra warmth provided by their clothes.

DISORIENTATION PRACTICE
The advanced practices are designed to simulate limb injury. They have the additional value of persuading the learner that drownproofing works! There only remains one other practice which may have a bearing on a real emergency situation.

It is fair to assume that anybody who finds himself involuntarily thrown into the water will either have entered

Figure 15   **Disorientation practice.**

the water from a height — the side of a ship — or will have been thrown upside down out of a capsizing boat. Learners enjoy playing with this idea. The following practices work with the above thoughts in mind.

1. The learner jumps into the water from the high diving board.
2. He jumps into the pool twisting as he does so.
3. He dives head first into the pool.
4. He dives into the water backwards in order to land on one shoulder.

All the above practices are best done fully dressed. With **constant supervision**, they may also be done when tied up.

5. One additional practice which some learners like to try involves their being blindfolded. The value of this exercise is that they can see how helpful it is to have eyes open.

CONCLUSION

At the end of a course of instruction a learner should be able to do the breathing cycle for prolonged periods without feeling fatigued. Most learners will be able to do the skill with one or more limbs immobilised. Even sinkers will have mastered a survival technique which will not cause them to be tired.

The keynote to success is perseverance and honest practice. Learners who think that treading water or floating on their back is easier are soon convinced otherwise if they try their methods in choppy water. It is easy to simulate choppy conditions in the swimming pool. I use a squad of a dozen boys leaping into the water continuously from three metres (nine feet). After that experience it is pleasant to get into the sea! It may be helpful to remind learners that it is far easier to float in salt water than in fresh water. All my comments about floating have referred to fresh water; but they apply with greater advantage in sea water.

5 The Travel Stroke

The drownproofers' motto is 'Economy and Simplicity'. The breathing cycle will be seen to be a highly economical way of staying afloat in water. This economy is carried over in the travel stroke. The simplicity of the travel stroke is that a drownproofer does not need to breathe as he moves.

The need for an economical travel stroke is less than that for an economical way of staying afloat. Most emergency situations do not require the ability to swim long distances. Organisations in the United States such as the Red Cross and the American Small Craft Association advise capsized boaters to remain with their craft in all circumstances for obvious reasons, although the immediate reaction in the event of a capsize if the shore seems near is to swim for it.

However, there may be circumstances requiring the ability to travel long distances in the water. Indeed it is not only those who capsize on a lake or in the sea who may need to be able to swim long distances. Leisure bathers are known frequently to swim 'out to an island', and find they have taken on more than they can manage. Others go into water when it is not safe to do so and find themselves rapidly exhausted by tides and currents. We are not merely concerned, then, with those who are far out to sea. And it must constantly be remembered that drownproofing is the only water skill which injured people can do for any length of time.

The travel stroke is designed to be done with a minimum expenditure of energy by fit as well as injured swimmers.

Travel rate is about 1½ kilometres (1 mile) per hour. A trained drownproofer can travel for long periods in moderately warm water. The implications of this are obvious.

1. At the end of the inhale stage of the breathing cycle (see Fig. 16a) the body will be going back into the vertical rest position of the breathing cycle.
2. As soon as the head is under water, tip it forward until it is face down. The hands should be brought up to the forehead and the legs readied for a scissor kick. The rear leg is going to do the work and the foot of that leg should be cocked almost to the surface of the water (16b).

Common Faults
- *The head is tipped forward too soon.*
- *The hands are brought up to the forehead too vigorously causing the rest of the body to sink.*
- *The rear leg is not sufficiently 'cocked'.*

3. The arms are extended above the head with the hands together. Immediately after, the top leg is kicked backwards and downwards until the feet are together. The learner is now gliding through the water (16c).

Common Faults
● *The arms are extended too forcibly above the head causing the drownproofer to go backwards and upset his rhythm.*
● *The kick is delivered too soon.*
● *The glide is not relaxed, and the learner is not looking down.*

4. As this first glide slows down, the arms are swept sideways until the hands touch the thighs (16d). The drownproofer now glides in the position shown in Fig. 16e. At this point start breathing out gently through the nose. The duration of the glide phases depend upon the individual. They can last from three to twenty seconds.

a

Figure 16   The travel stroke.
a   The end of the breathing cycle.

41

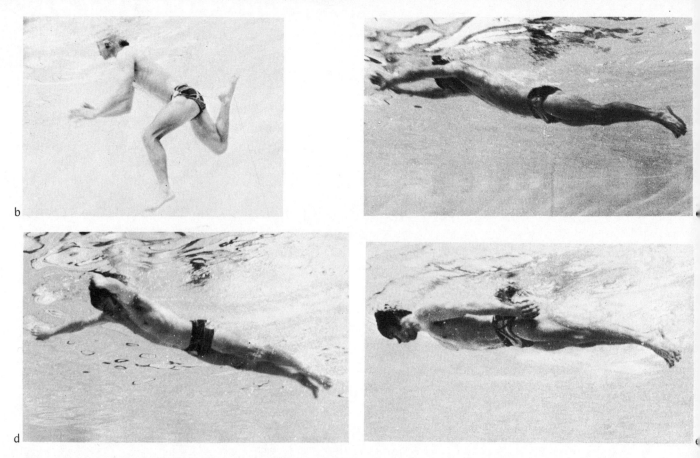

b

d

42

f

g

b   Preparing to shoot the arms above the head and to kick with the
top leg.
c   The leg glide phase.
d   The arm pull.
e   The final glide phase.
f   Preparing to breathe. The legs are being brought up to the chest,
and the arms starting to hang.
g   The knees are tucked up to the chest to assist regaining the vertical
rest position.

h

h   The vertical rest position nearly regained prior to resuming the full breathing cycle.

Common Faults
- *The arm sweep is started too soon. It must work separately from the leg kick so that the maximum glide time is achieved.*
- *The neck is not relaxed and the hip is bent.*
- *Breathing problems occur at this stage.*

5. Towards the end of the glide most learners will find themselves at the surface of the water. Good floaters will have difficulty in resuming the vertical rest position and should start to exhale earlier.

6. At the end of the glide both knees are brought up to the chest and the back is rounded (16f and 16g). The vertical rest position can then be resumed (16h). At this stage the breathing cycle is done in the normal way and the travel cycle repeated.

7. Repeat the travel cycle and breathing cycle continuously. The learner should attempt two lengths of the swimming pool at the outset. Thereafter the ideal is any distance up to 1000 metres.

Common Faults
- *The learner breathes in as he travels by lifting his head. In rough seas he will take in water. Correct this by doing two or three breathing cycles between each travel stroke.*
- *The sequence of movements becomes confused and the learner forgets part of the cycle. Demonstrate the movement*

again and ask the learner to repeat it to you verbally before re-attempting it. The learner must think about what he is doing.

- *There is no pause between the kick and the pull.*
- *The learner holds on to his breath too long.*
- *He does not relax during the glide.*
- *He breathes before the trunk is vertical.*
- *He exhales too little or too much during the glide.*
- *He does not empty his lungs completely during the exhale.*

Good floaters will probably start to breathe out earlier than poor floaters. As with the breathing cycle individuals vary in the amount of air they like to release during the glide phase. Because of this the travel stroke should not be attempted until the breathing cycle has been mastered and the learner has control over his breathing. Trial and error will decide what is best for each individual. It is important that there are no leaks of air until exhalation is begun. It is worth emphasising to learners that they should breathe in and out when it suits them, and they should never be completely out of air. Any distress experienced during the glide phases will interfere with the next breathing cycle.

The discomfort felt during the initial stages of the breathing cycle is magnified during the glide stages of the travel stroke. Lungs feel as if they are bursting and the head sings. *Everybody* feels this sensation at first. The remedy is the same as before. Persevere. The causes of the misery are many.

The drownproofer is not relaxed and hence oxygen is going to tensed muscles. He may have breathed in too much air during the breathing cycle. He is holding on to the glide too long, too soon. He is not allowing enough air to escape while he glides. He is allowing too little air to escape. It is important that the teacher knows all the possible symptoms and that he warns the learners that they will feel uncomfortable to start with.

Apart from breathing control, emphasis should be given to the control of movement. The teacher should ensure that each individual is doing the cycle in the correct sequence. It is sometimes difficult to persuade learners to persevere with the skill since it is, at first, contradictory to their instincts and training.

Do not labour the travel stroke too much. The most common reaction from novices will be that it is 'easier' to do the breast stroke. They will continue to believe this until they have mastered the travel stroke. Do not allow them to use the breast stroke leg kick at this stage.

PROGRESSIONS

Pupils who have learnt the classic Lanoue technique will wish to experiment with their own techniques. It will be commonly found that many of them favour a breast stroke leg kick. Allow them to use this provided they do not convert the whole into a breast stroke. It is worthwhile pausing to think why everybody regards the breast stroke or the side stroke as the least tiring strokes — in any distance swim you will rarely see any other stroke used. In breast stroke only the head comes out of the water, and in side stroke nothing comes out. Emphasise this point and link it up to our continual emphasis on gentle, relaxed movements.

1. Partly immobilise the subject. Complete immobilisation does not make for effective travelling. A person so badly handicapped is best advised to remain stationary doing the breathing cycle.
2. Experimentation with a personal method of travel which is consistent with the 'stop to breathe' rule is desirable at this stage.
3. Do the skill while fully clothed.

A FINAL POINT

In any genuine survival situation a swimmer, whether he is trained to drownproof or not, will automatically use strokes which appear to be getting him out of difficulty quickly. The idea of 'doing' is central to many deaths. If the drownproofing training has been thorough the swimmer will realise that he is 'doing' something even during the static, unspectacular breathing cycle. What he is doing is saving his own life by using a simple, logical technique. But a strong swimmer who has decided to 'swim for it' will probably strike out in front crawl. As he tires he will, perhaps, change to breast stroke, thence to back stroke, thence to side stroke. All the while, and this attitude is seen among schoolchildren doing a distance swim, he will be changing his technique because he believes that a change is as good as a rest. I do not want to argue the nonsense of that here. Suffice it to say that if he has the drownproofing travel stroke among his battery of skills, he is likely to use that during his swim. This is itself a valuable addition. It is a far, far better thing for him to drownproof all the time if there is any doubt as to the success or otherwise of his emergency swim.

6 Drownproofing for Special Cases

The previous chapters have alluded to special difficulties which various categories of people encounter in the water. In this chapter we look at the modifications to the technique which these people will have to make.

SINKERS

A sinker is a person who, having taken a full breath, has gone under water with his legs beneath him, propelled himself to the surface so that he can feel cold air on the back of his neck, and still sinks.

The reason for sinking is physical: fat and air float while bone and muscle sink (see p. 13). The displacement of fat around the body determines whether a person will float and in what position — as we have already seen, men and women usually float in different positions as a result of diferent dispositions of fat and air. There are very few sinkers among women and only slightly more among men. However, a good floater can turn himself into a sinker by donning a weight belt. He will soon realise just how difficult are the problems which all sinkers face.

Ironically, many of our best swimmers tend to sink as a result of their training which has caused them to become muscular. Their superb conditioning allows them to travel great distances without fatigue, even though there is virtually no resting phase while they swim. But in extreme conditions such as injury or cold, these swimmers will be glad of a more restful technique. It should not be forgotten that even the best swimmers can fall victim to tides and currents.

The difference between sinking and floating is often just a mouthful of air. People who think they are sinkers can try a simple test. They should fill their lungs with air — and then breathe in even more. If, after this, they still do not float, they are sinkers. Often, though, those who think they are sinkers suffer from a technical rather than a physiological problem.

THE TECHNIQUE FOR SINKERS
1. The sinker's shoulders and chin should be in the water during the breathing cycle as with any other drownproofer.
2. As the forearms come up to the forehead the sinker straddles his legs so that the sole of the front foot and top of the rear foot 'hold' on the water (Fig. 17, stages 1 and 2).

3. As the head is **gently** lifted and the arms swept sideways the legs kick down firmly on the water (stage 3). The combined arm and leg action should give the sinker time to breathe. This technique is the same as that used for floaters except that floaters, after a little practice do not need to use their legs. At this point the legs are together.
4. After the head has gone under the water it is tipped forward. At the same time the sinker does another compensatory leg kick to prevent himself from sinking too far under the water (stage 4).
5. The cycle is repeated. Essentially the sinker does three kicks per cycle. He kicks to prevent himself from going too deep at the end of the inhalation. He kicks as his arms sweep outwards during the breathing cycle, and he kicks again at the end of the breathing phase.

Common Faults
● *Allowing the body to sink too far under the water. To correct this, start the compensatory leg kick even before the head is submerged. If necessary do more than one kick. Each kick should be gentle.*
● *Coming too high out of the water to breathe indicates that a more gentle leg and arm action is needed.*

1

Figure 17   **The breathing cycle for sinkers.**

2   3   4

1   2   3   4

If after trying these practices the sinker is still unable to stay afloat without great effort he must use the travel stroke permanently. This will be less exhausting than treading water. It will be to his advantage if at the end sweep of the arms in the breathing cycle, he holds his arms out to the sides (Fig. 18, stage 1).

MODIFIED TRAVEL STROKE FOR THE SINKER

The difference between the travelling technique for the sinker and that for the good floater is small. The sinker can help himself if he holds his arms out to the side, but will find that he cannot glide as far as the floater without sinking. He may have to do extra leg kicks as described above. Provided he keeps on the move he should have no difficulty.

5   6   7   8   9

The diagram (Fig. 18) shows that the sinker starts his breathing cycle as soon as the legs begin to sink. He has no rest period here, but provided he is relaxed during the glide phase and his arms are close by his sides he should be able to rest as he glides. It is important to the sinker that he does not allow air to leak during the glide.

Figure 18   **The modified travel stroke for sinkers.**

HIGHLY EFFICIENT FLOATERS

Some people, particularly women, have difficulty in doing this technique because they float too well. Under most circumstances this is to their great advantage. It is arguable that because of their 'built-in' buoyancy there will never be any need for them to drownproof. The only advantage in the skill for them is that there may be occasions when floating on their backs causes breathing problems. There is no doubt that the face down position is a more natural floating position. However, with good floaters the body, even when face down, is horizontal. This means that they have difficulty in putting their head in the water. During the breathing cycle this causes them to become breathless. To help them become vertical they should breathe out more fully during the exhale. If they are not vertical during the inhale stage the neck is forced back by the water so that the floater must crane it back even further in order to breathe in. The effort involved in having to work thus uneconomically has already been discussed (p. 15). During the travel phase the good floater must breathe out fully during the glide and force his knees up to his chest in order to become vertical. Any arm action during the breathing cycle must be very, very gentle, or the floater will find the high position of the trunk and legs at one end of the body, plus the high position of the torso and head caused by the arm action, most uncomfortable.

THE PHYSICALLY HANDICAPPED

There are many and varied specialist considerations concerning swimming for the physically handicapped. All that can be said of a general nature is that many diseases cause wasting away of skeletal muscle which means the swimmer is more buoyant. This 'advantage' is offset by the fact that such muscular atrophy means that the handicapped person is more susceptible to cold. Furthermore the floating position of limbless people is considerably different from the 'norm'.

Whatever methods are advocated for teaching the physically handicapped to swim, we can be sure that we will not achieve our aim if the learners do not have a basic understanding of buoyancy and propulsion. Once these principles are understood the individual can adapt them to suit his own needs. Successful drownproofing relies entirely on this understanding. This is a far more constructive approach than simply trying to adapt orthodox swimming strokes to the handicapped.

Drownproofing is probably the best way to approach the physically handicapped. The economy of effort required for its accomplishment will be beneficial to the swimmer who will already be coping with problems of poor circulation or of cold. However, insufficient work has yet been done on drownproofing for the handicapped to allow discussion of the problems involved here.

NON-SWIMMING ADULTS

There seems to be an increasing number of adults who wish to learn to swim. Their immediate need is safety and confidence. This can be achieved through a course in drownproofing.

The main advantage in teaching a non-swimming adult over teaching a child is that the adult is differently motivated from the outset. Children want to be able to move in the water. Adults understand the principles behind successful swimming and can apply their understanding to the problem in hand. Furthermore it is often necessary to start adults in the deep end because their weight and height does not allow them to feel, or be, buoyant in a metre of water, nor are there any helpful buoyancy aids on the market for them. Traditional swimming techniques rely upon a person's ability to float. Drownproofing relies on flotation just as much but emphasises it in a different way. Thus, because drownproofing is a simpler skill to learn, and because an adult is concerned with safety first and movement after, it seems best to teach drownproofing first. Traditional techniques can come later.

There are some people who would disagree with this. To those I would say that the sight of an infant kicking his way across a pool in arm bands is not that of watching him swim. He is not 'swimming'. The child loves doing it and it is a marvellous vicarious experience for the teacher. The same situation applied to an adult is ludicrous. The adult knows that if his buoyancy is efficient he will float and, then, 'swim'. The use of aids for the child is to give him an understanding of the concept of 'buoyancy'. The adult already has that concept but must apply it to himself.

Starting with a demonstration of the mushroom float and going on through the gamut of floating practices referred to earlier will enable the adult to see what is required. It is easy for the adult to be supervised in the water. Many pools have a 'sill' on which the teacher can stand in arm's reach of the learner. Besides which, we all tend to forget that there is for all of us a moment of water truth; we have to take the vital plunge on our own. The child who has had the volume of air reduced in his arm bands week by week has still to cast them off for ever, and trust in his training. We cannot teach a person to swim by doing it for him. I believe that by emphasising that the lungs are air bags, that the water will hold us up, that whatever we do there is a point at which we sink slightly, many of the problems of learners can be overcome.

SAILORS AND CANOEISTS

All sailors and canoeists should learn to drownproof, if only because many people die each year because they fail to wear their lifejacket or buoyancy aids. The type of lifejacket which turns a person onto his back and holds his head high out of the water offers a capsized person a greater chance of survival than does drownproofing. However, there are many buoyancy aids on the market which, as their name suggests, give and need some help. It is very pleasant to drownproof in them. The technique is the same as that for average floaters except that all limb movements must be done much more gently. Those who advocate swimming on the back while wearing these aids should try to hold the supine position for any length of time in choppy water! The advantages of the drownproofer's breathing technique is soon apparent. Tests I have carried out on eight different types of buoyancy aid have shown that a swimmer is automatically turned onto his front by them, from whatever position he enters the water. In many cases the waistcoat-type aid tipped the wearer too far forward such that he could not breathe at all without fighting hard to counteract his buoyancy!

It must be clearly remembered that drownproofing is one extra survival skill; it is not a replacement for regular swimming or for existing water safety programmes. I believe and have tried to show clearly the advantages it has over all other methods. However, there are many vital aspects of safety training which I have not mentioned. Below is a list of activities and core of knowledge which would seem to be invaluable to all those who go on, in, under, through or near water.

The individual skills detailed below are ones which I have found valuable while teaching 'swimming' to children of these ages. Individual achievements will vary, but a hint will have been given of where drownproofing skills can fit in to the swimming lesson. Remember our criteria are safety first, challenge second.

1. *For the very young* (under 6's)
   Move freely in chest deep water.
   Submerge and hold breath.
   Turn over backwards, forwards or roll sideways.
   Breath control by bobbing around in the water.
   Float face down in a wide and narrow position.
   Front and back glide.

Course of Drownproofing

Jump into chest-deep water.
Swim five metres.
Drownproof, tread water or swim in place for 30 seconds.
Answer simple questions on water safety.

2. *Beginners* (6—8)
  Reaching assists.
  Jump into deep water.
  Tread water for 1 minute.
  Drownproof for 1 minute.
  Swim 15 metres on front.
  Swim 10 metres on back.

3. *Juniors* (9—11)
  Resuscitation.
  Front dive into deep water.
  50 metres on front and 50 metres on back to be done continuously.
  Tread water for 1 minute and drownproof for 3 minutes, to be done continuously.
  Water safety knowledge.

4. *Intermediate* (under 13)
  Water safety knowledge.
  Surface dive followed by 5 metre under-water swim.
  200 metre continuous swim comprising 50 metres each of front crawl, side stroke, breast stroke and back stroke.
  On back: 25 metres sculling followed by 25 metres life saving leg kick.
  Drownproof for 5 minutes.

5. *Senior* (under 16)
  In the water resuscitation.
  300 metre continuous swim comprising 75 metres each of the four strokes above.
  75 metres life saving leg kick.
  Drownproof for 10 minutes.
  Travel stroke 50 metres.
  Shallow water entry, feet first.
  (All the above to be done fully dressed.)

6. *Advanced* (16—18)
  Candidates must be fully dressed.
  Drownproof for 10 minutes with hands and feet tied.
  1½ kilometre travel stroke.